T.W.VOTER

This book tells about hunting dinosaurs with a whisk broom; about the Thunder Lizard, which weighed 80,000 pounds; about armored dinosaurs, flying dragons, and sea serpents that lived 100 million years ago.

Here is a first-hand account of world-famous expeditions to the Gobi Desert, in northeastern Asia, to search for fossil remains of dinosaurs.

Dr. Roy Chapman Andrews, who died in 1960, was not only a scientist-explorer but also Director of the American Museum of Natural History.

ALL ABOUT DINOSAURS

ALL ABOUT DINOSAURS

By Roy Chapman Andrews

Illustrated by Thomas W. Voter

allabout
books

RANDOM HOUSE
NEW YORK

The Library of Congress Cataloguing in Publication Information
is located on the rear endpaper.

12348

This book is affectionately dedicated to
KITTY AND TOMMY BELL

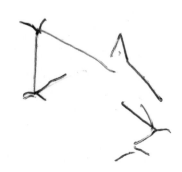

CONTENTS

INTRODUCING DINOSAURS

Dinosaurs were the strangest animals that ever existed on this earth. They were the sort of creatures you might think of as inhabiting another planet or the kind you dream of in a bad nightmare. The word dinosaur (*die'-no-sawr*) means "terrible lizard." It is a good description. Dinosaurs were reptiles, cold-blooded animals related to crocodiles, snakes and lizards. At one time they ruled the entire world.

Some were of gigantic size, heavier than a dozen elephants. Those had long snake-like necks, small heads, and twenty-foot tails. They waded along the margins of lakes and rivers, half sunk in mud and water, feeding on soft plants.

Others walked on powerful hind legs, and stood as tall as a palm tree. Their small arms ended in clutching hands and curved claws longer than those of the biggest bear. Their mouths were more than a yard deep, bristling with great dagger-like teeth. They killed other dinosaurs and tore the flesh off their bodies, gulping it in hundred-pound chunks.

Some were huge, pot-bellied reptiles thirty feet long. They walked erect, balanced by heavy tails. Their faces were drawn out and flattened into wide, horny beaks like a duck's bill. Two thousand small teeth filled their mouths. They loved to wallow in lake-shore mud, chewing plants and herbs. But they were good swimmers, too. When a hungry flesh-eater leaped out of the forest, they dashed for deep water where he couldn't follow.

Other dinosaurs were short-legged and square-bodied, as big as an army tank. Long horns projected forward like two machine guns from a bony shield over an ugly hooked beak. They lumbered through the jungle, and all other animals fled in terror.

Another fantastic reptile carried a line of triangular plates down the middle of its back. On the tip of the ten-foot tail were four huge spikes, three feet long. At the same time there lived a dinosaur completely armored by a heavy shell. Its thick tail ended in a huge mass of bone. He could swing it like a war club and give a crushing blow.

Some dinosaurs were slender and swift, skipping over the plains faster than a race horse. And some were very small, no larger than rabbits. They hid among the rocks or in the thickest forest for protection.

What I tell you about these unbelievable creatures is true. They really did live. We know they did because we find their bones buried in the earth. These bones have been fossilized or turned to stone.

The impression of an ancient plant is seen in this stone.

All About Dinosaurs

Also we find their footprints in stone. It is just as if you had stepped in soft mud, and the tracks your feet made had become solid rock. In the same way the impressions of plants and trees and insects have been preserved in stone. So we know what the country was like when the dinosaurs lived.

The time was the Age of Reptiles. That was a period in the earth's history which began 200 million years in the past and ended 60 million years ago. When we talk about millions of years, it is difficult to get a real mind-picture of that vast length of time. Ape-like human beings did not exist until one million years ago. Our recorded history is hardly 7,000 years old. The time back to the Age of Reptiles is like the distance in miles separating us from the moon.

People often ask if there are any dinosaurs living today. The answer is, no. They all died out at the end of the Age of Reptiles. Why they disappeared we don't know. We only know they did. When you see pictures in the "funnies" of dinosaurs with men, that is all imagination. No human being ever saw a dinosaur alive. They had become extinct 60 million years before man came upon the earth.

The Age of Reptiles lasted 140 million years. During that great length of time dinosaurs ruled the land. In the

Man has lived only a short time in the earth's history.

air weird goblin-like reptiles sailed through the gloomy skies. Some of them had long faces, peaked heads and twenty-foot wings. They make one think of fairy-tale witches flying on broomsticks.

The oceans swarmed with other reptiles. There were great sea serpents with wide flat bodies, long slender necks, and small heads filled with sharp teeth. There were also giant lizards, forty feet long, and others that looked like fish. Truly the land, the sea and the air were frightening in the Age of Reptiles.

But the earth back in that far dim past was not as it is today. The climate was different. In most places it was tropical or sub-tropical like southern California or southern Florida. The climate was the same almost everywhere. There were no cold winters. If there had been, the reptiles could not have flourished the way they did. They didn't like cold weather. In those days the weather was warm and humid the year round. Thick jungles, low lands and swamps stretched across most of the world.

In the Age of Reptiles the great mountain systems had not yet been born. The Himalayas, now the highest mountain range in the world, did not exist. There were no Rocky Mountains. Instead, the low lying country of western America and of central Europe held great inland seas. What is now the state of Kansas was covered with water. Also Wyoming and Montana. The land lifted at times and sank and rose again. One hundred and forty million years is a long time, and many changes took place.

Our geography books would not have been of much use then. The continents then were not as they are today. There were land connections which do not exist at the present time. North America and Asia doubtless had a wide land bridge across the Bering Straits. North and South America were more broadly united than today. Possibly North America and Europe were joined across Greenland and Iceland. Europe and Africa were connected where the Mediterranean Sea now separates them. Asia and Australia were joined by land in what is now the East Indies.

This is the way we think the world geography looked during much of the Age of Reptiles. You can see, therefore, that animals could have traveled from one continent to another. They were not cut off by the climate, mountains and oceans that exist today.

That is the reason why dinosaur bones are found over much of the world. They have been discovered in North and South America from Canada to Patagonia, in various parts of Europe, in Africa and Asia, and even in Australia.

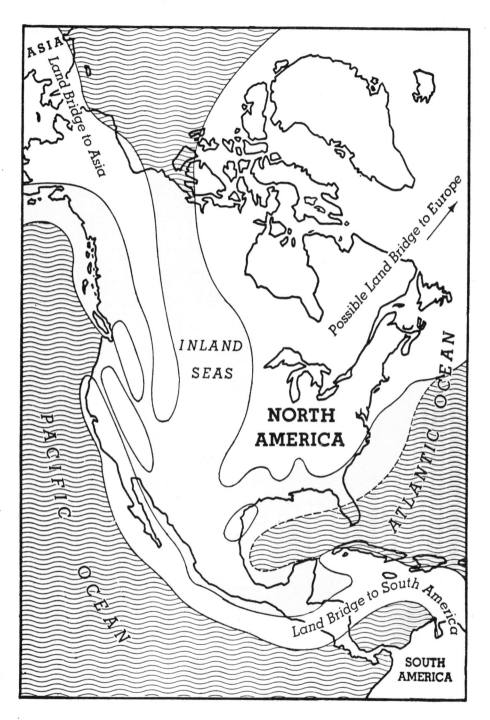

In the Age of Reptiles world geography was very different.

THE DISCOVERY OF DINOSAURS

Scientists had been digging up the fossilized remains of other animals for some years before dinosaurs were discovered. The first ever found, or at least recorded, was unearthed at East Windsor, Connecticut, in 1818. No one knew to what creature the bones belonged.

Years later Professor Marsh gave them the name An-chisaurus (*An'-key-sawr'-us*).

In 1822, the wife of Dr. Gideon Mantell discovered some peculiar teeth in the rocks of Sussex, England. No one at that time had ever heard of a dinosaur. Dr. Mantell sent the teeth to several other scientists. At first they said the teeth belonged to a rhinoceros.

That didn't seem right to Mantell, and he went back to the place where the teeth had been found. There he dug up a number of bones. He studied them for a long time.

Finally he decided they represented a new type of large reptile. He described and named it Iguanodon (*Ig-wan'-o-don*) because the teeth looked like those of the living iguana lizard.

But it was Sir Richard Owen who recognized that these extinct reptiles needed a general name. He called them dinosaurs, meaning "terrible lizards."

Strangely enough one of the first discoverers of fossil reptiles was not a scientist but a young girl, named Mary Anning. She lived on the coast of southern England. She used to help her father hunt for fossil sea shells. These they sold to tourists who came to the village in the summer.

In 1811, when Mary was twelve years old, she made a great discovery. It was the petrified skeleton of a reptile that lived in the sea when dinosaurs ruled the land. It was quite unknown. The animal was named Ichthyosaurus (*Ik'-thee-o-sawr'-us*).

Iguanadon was the dinosaur first described by Dr. Mantell.

Mary's reptile created great excitement among scientists. She searched the rocks near her home and found other petrified marine or sea animals. When her father died, she went into the business of fossil collecting.

In 1821, Mary Anning unearthed the first skeleton of a sea serpent which was named Plesiosaurus (*Plees'-i-o-sawr'-us*). Seven years later she made another important discovery. It was the skeleton of a pterodactyl (*ter-o-dack'-til*), a flying reptile. This was the first of its kind ever known from England. Mary Anning made quite a little money selling the fossils to museums all over the world. Her name became famous in science.

Dinosaurs not only left their bones in the rocks; they also left their footprints. The Connecticut Valley has some of the best preserved dinosaur tracks in the world.

In 1802, a farmer named Pliny Moody, ploughed up a block of stone. It showed small imprints like those of a bird's feet. These were called the tracks of Noah's raven. People let it go at that. Others were found, but no one paid much attention to them until 1835.

Then Professor Hitchcock of Amherst College studied them and decided they had been made by large extinct birds. Not until later was it understood that they were the tracks of dinosaurs that walked on their hind

Mary Anning found the first fossil reptile in 1811.

legs. Professor Hitchcock's mistake was quite natural. Dinosaurs were almost unknown at that time, and the three-toed footprints look very much like those of birds.

The Connecticut dinosaur tracks are very, very old. They were made about 200 million years ago at the beginning of the Age of Reptiles.

The face of Connecticut has changed much since those dim dark days. It was not beautiful then as it is now.

The landscape was all dull green. There was little vegetation except conifers, ferns, and cycads (*cy'-kads*) which are trees something like palms and ferns. Not a single flower gave color to the forests. There were no brilliant tints of autumn leaves in October. Neither were there birds. Turtles swam in the ponds, lizards slept in the sun, and small dinosaurs skipped about in unbelievable millions.

The story of the Connecticut tracks is an important chapter in the history of dinosaurs. That part of the Connecticut River Valley, where the footprints are found, was an ancient river bed. Or it may have been a long shallow arm of the sea. Its water level changed greatly. Large stretches would be left dry to bake in the sun for days or weeks. Then suddenly they would be covered with muddy water.

For some reason, dinosaurs liked to come to this river flat. When they walked across it, their feet sank into the soft mud and left deep imprints. Then the mud dried up and baked in the sun. When the flats were again covered with water, sediment filled the tracks and made casts. After many years the mud became hard rock.

Thousands of tracks have been preserved in this way. Dinosaurs must have been there in millions. Their foot-

These small dinosaur tracks were found in Connecticut.

prints show they were of many different kinds and sizes. The largest tracks are fifteen inches long and three feet apart. They were made by really big dinosaurs which walked on their hind feet. Probably the animals had small front limbs like those of a kangaroo. This seems to be true, because there are impressions of dinosaur "hind ends" where they sat down to rest. With these are casts of the smaller forelegs in just the right position where they touched the ground.

It is strange that very few bones of these reptiles have been found. Probably the rocks containing their skeletons lie out to sea. The bodies must have been carried away by tides or currents before they had time to be buried and fossilized on land.

Connecticut is by no means the only place where dinosaur footprints have been found. Texas, Montana and other states can boast of bigger and better tracks but not so many as in Connecticut. About 1830, in England, dinosaur footprints were discovered in rocks of the same age as those in Connecticut. But no bones of the reptiles that made them have been discovered. For some reason these tracks all go from west to east. Perhaps the dinosaurs were migrating or traveling a regular road to their feeding grounds. Belgium, too, has some very fine tracks of the big Iguanodon, the same type of dinosaur that Dr. Mantell described.

At first, most fossils were found only by accident. When digging the foundations of a house, making a road, or getting slate out of a quarry, men would turn up strange bones. They would take them home, and their families would keep them as curiosities for a while. Eventually some of the bones would be presented to a museum where they were studied by scientists.

Year by year, interest grew in the past life of the earth. It was slow because most people think only about what happens this year or what will happen next year. That seems more important than anything that happened fifty, or a hundred or a thousand years ago. But some of them knew that you can't understand the present, unless you learn what went on in the past. Scientists realized that fossil bones and plants are pages from the history of the earth. They were written in stone instead of words on paper, but they could tell a true story just the same.

So more and more scientific men began studying fossils. They found it very exciting. It was like a detective novel. They had to piece together the strange, unreal life of the world millions of years ago. They did it from the impressions of plants left in the rocks, from fossil bones, and from insects, and bits of petrified wood.

A detective does the same thing when he starts to solve the mystery of a robbery or a murder. He finds a handkerchief, a bit of ribbon or a shred of clothing. Those are his clews. He puts them all together, and they begin to form a pattern in his mind. With a little imagination he thinks he knows what happened. So he takes his evidence into court.

That is the way a scientist works when he tries to reconstruct the prehistoric world. He studies the bones and the plants and the fossilized wood. He decides what the climate was like and the vegetation and the sort of ani-

The pterodactyl was a flying reptile in dinosaur days.

mals that lived there. He presents his case to other scientists. Perhaps his evidence isn't good enough for them to agree he is right. So he just waits. He hopes that after a while more evidence will be discovered in the rocks to prove his case.

I know how exciting it is because I am one of the detectives who have been collecting the fossil evidence. Never in my life have I done anything more fascinating.

All About Dinosaurs

You can do it, too, if you will only keep your eyes open when you prowl around rocks. Perhaps you may find a dinosaur bone or some other fossil. Mary Anning did it when she discovered some of the first sea serpents. She made herself famous.

Until after the Civil War, people in America were busy trying to preserve the union of the states. They didn't think much about anything else. But when peace came, their attention turned to our great western country. The U.S. Government sent out exploring parties. Usually they had geologists with them, for they wanted to find out about minerals and other things in the earth. These men discovered hundreds of fossil bones and many dinosaurs. Thus began the organized work of collecting fossils in America.

The study of fossils is called paleontology (*pay-lee-on-tol'-o-gy*). The word means "the science of ancient living beings." Two American paleontologists were very important at that time. One was Professor Edward D. Cope of Philadelphia. The other was Professor O. C. Marsh of Yale University. Both were rich men. Between the years 1870 and 1895, they sent out their own collecting parties. Those went to the Great Plains and the Rocky Mountain basins. They found that the badlands of Wyoming and Montana were filled with fossils. Many dinosaur skeletons were discovered.

But it was dangerous work in those early years. Indians were still on the warpath in places. A collector might be walking along the side of a ravine with his eyes on the ground. An Indian could easily sneak up and send an arrow or a rifle bullet into his body. Still the work went on.

At first Cope and Marsh were friends. Later they became rivals and bitter enemies. It was a race with them to see who could get the most fossil animals and name them. We know now that it was a foolish race. There are enough fossils for everybody in that vast country.

But it had many good results. One of them was to get scientists in other countries more keenly interested and start them to work. Also, museums began to send expeditions for fossil collecting all over the world. That is how I happened to go to Asia, to the Gobi Desert of Mongolia. I went for the American Museum of Natural History in New York. There I did my first fossil hunting and found my first dinosaur.

HOW FOSSILS ARE MADE

I have been talking about fossils without explaining what they are, or how they are formed. The name comes from the Latin word *fossilis*, which means "dug up." Therefore, a fossil must have been buried at some time. It is the remains of a plant or an animal that once lived upon the earth.

Fossils are being made today just as they were a million years ago. A bone your dog has buried in the ground may some day become a fossil if it remains long enough.

All About Dinosaurs

When an animal dies, there is a great chance that its skeleton will be pulled apart by other animals and destroyed. But that doesn't always happen. Sometimes wind may cover it quickly with sand, or rain may wash mud over it. This heaps up higher and higher. Water, which contains minerals in solution, drips through it. Then a very slow change takes place. Particle by particle the animal

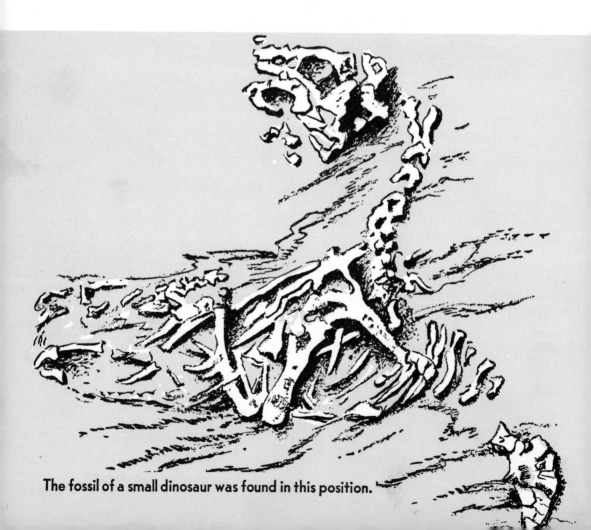

The fossil of a small dinosaur was found in this position.

matter in the bone is replaced by mineral matter. So it is petrified or "turned to stone."

This change may be rapid or very slow. It depends upon conditions. A bone may be completely petrified in a few hundred years if the water is heavy with minerals. Or it may lie for thousands of years without being entirely mineralized. Then it is called a "sub-fossil." Most often bones are changed to sandstone or limestone. But sometimes they are formed by unusual minerals such as iron or even opal.

In the Gobi Desert we discovered the skeleton of a dinosaur in the side of a cliff. It was in an iron deposit, and the bones had been completely changed to iron.

Quite often an animal may die on the bank of a stream or in the water. The body floats along until it comes to rest on a sand bank or in a backwater. There it sinks to the bottom. The flesh decays, and the bones are gently covered with very fine mud. It fills every groove and pore and preserves the mark of each ridge or furrow. After a long while the sediment is pressed together into rock. The stream dries up or changes its course. The bones are left enclosed in stone, perhaps to be found by some fossil hunter millions of years later.

Some parts of the skeleton are more frequently preserved than others. Because they are hard and solid, skulls and teeth are often found when nothing else is present. Leg and arm bones and ribs are easily broken. Very rarely the flesh, skin or tendons are entirely or partly preserved. In such cases, the soft parts were protected in some way from decay, and mineralization was very rapid.

Quite often fossils are formed as molds, or casts, like the dinosaur tracks from Connecticut that I described. In the Gobi Desert we found impressions of plants and insects in what are called "paper-shales." These were made from extremely fine sediment, deposited in horizontal layers, which separate into sheets as thin as paper. In one is the perfect imprint of a mosquito. In another the imprint of a butterfly's wing is so beautifully preserved that you can see the most delicate veins under a magnifying glass.

These paper-shales were formed in sheltered pools of quiet water. Leaves or insects which died upon the surface sank to the bottom and were gently covered with a blanket of the finest mud. As the animal matter decayed, their tiny bodies left a perfect impression in the mud. It was exactly like the mold that one makes in plaster.

This is fossilized wood in the petrified forest of Arizona.

Mary Anning was hunting for fossil sea shells when she discovered the first marine reptile in England. These were actually the casts of shells. The shells were pressed down into the mud. After a while all the animal matter was dissolved by the water. But a hole, or mold, was left where the shell had been. Later this mold was filled with sediment which hardened into a cast of the shell. We have found casts of the birds' eggs. Often the kernels of nuts are fossilized. Many of the small animals, like crabs, that lived in the sea or swamps have been preserved.

Most of you have seen fossilized wood. In Arizona there is a place called the "petrified forest" where hundreds of fallen trees lie on the ground. Some are great trunks thirty or forty feet long. Chips and chunks are scattered about. The vegetable matter in the wood has been replaced by minerals. So completely was it done that, with a microscope, you can see the cellular structure of the wood.

The impressions of leaves, of seeds, and of wood tell an important story. From them it is easy to decide what the vegetation was like when those plants and trees lived. We can even know the climate. If the trees were of desert type, there must have been little rainfall. If they were those of the tropics, like palms, certainly the weather was warm with much rain. So you see how the history of past life on the earth has been written in the rocks. You can read it easily, once you have learned the language.

Of course fossils can only be preserved in sedimentary rocks like sandstone, limestone, slate and shale. These rocks are made up of small particles of sediment pressed together. You couldn't find fossils in granite or volcanic

Fossils are often found in ravines, gulleys and canyons.

rocks which have been formed by heat and change. So
when we go fossil hunting, we first have to know that
we are on sedimentary rocks.

Next, the surface must be cut up into ravines and gullies and canyons. Thus we have a cross section of the
land. Usually it is desert or dry country with little grass,
trees, or other vegetation to protect the soil from the
wind and weather. Rain and "flash floods" cut deep gullies in the surface. These expose the bones that may lie
buried underneath.

All About Dinosaurs

A cake is a good example of what I mean. If it is covered with frosting, you don't know what kind of a cake it is. It may be a plain cake or a layer cake, or it may contain raisins or nuts. But if you slice through it, then you can tell. If nuts or raisins are there, you probably will see some of them in the cross section from top to bottom.

That is what ravines and gullies and canyons do for the fossil hunter. They give him a cross section of the land. He walks along the sides of the ravines or in a dry river bed. Some bones will probably show if they have been buried there, just as the nuts and raisins show in the cake.

It is quite useless to dig for fossils unless there is some indication that bones are there. You just can't go out and say: "Here I will dig for a fossil. I hope I'll find one." No, you must look for bits of bone, for discolorations in the rock, for something that will show that a fossil might be there. When we were in the Gobi Desert, we traveled for hundreds of miles across sedimentary rocks. We knew fossils might lie underneath the surface, but there was no place where we had a cross section of the land. Finally we found it, and then we discovered the first fossils ever known in Mongolia.

HUNTING DINOSAURS
WITH A WHISK BROOM

Many of the animals of Europe and America are related. Some are as close as first cousins. It seemed probable, therefore, that their ancestors came from the same place. That place might well be Asia because it lies between Europe and America. But before 1922 very little was known of the fossil history of Central Asia. It was time to find out something about it. So in 1922 I organized an expedition to go to the great plateau of Mongolia.

All About Dinosaurs

As you can imagine, a desert is the best place in which
to hunt fossils. That is because it has little vegetation to
cover the top of the ground. The greatest desert in Asia
is the Gobi. It stretches east and west through the center
of Mongolia for 2,000 miles. A thirsty land; a land of
desolation! Bitterly cold in winter; burning hot in summer! A gravel desert with only stunted sage brush,
clumps of wire-like grass, and thorny bushes! Gazelles,

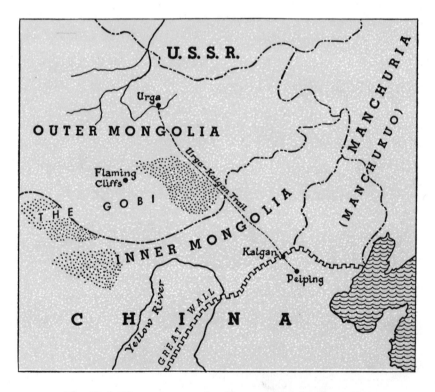

The Gobi Desert occupies the center of Mongolia.

wild asses, and wolves ranged the marching sands. Mongols, some of whom had never seen a white man, were the only people. Few explorers had been there, and they brought back tales of thirst, cold, and hunger.

I believed the desert could be conquered with automobiles which would give fast transportation. We could work in the summer and return before winter. Others thought we were crazy to take motor cars on such an exploration. Only camels had been used in that country. No fossils ever had been found in the Gobi except one rhinoceros tooth. It was a great gamble, but that made it more interesting.

So, with some of the world's best scientists, we went to the Gobi. We had forty men, eight motor cars, and 150 camels to carry gasoline and supplies. It was the biggest land scientific expedition ever to leave the United States. We were not only hunting fossils. Part of our program was to collect the living birds, animals, and plants and to map the country.

We started from the little frontier town of Kalgan, north of Peking (Peiping), China. Kalgan is at the edge of the great Mongolian plateau. The land rises quickly, and the road goes up through a pass 4,500 feet high. The trail was very bad. Deep ruts had been cut by the spike-studded wheels of Chinese carts. Mud holes and huge rocks made it an "automobile nightmare." Every few miles we had to stop to cool the engines.

Wonderful views spread out below us as we climbed higher. We looked back over thousands of canyons, ravines and gullies to purple mountains in the far distance. On the ridge above, stretched the Great Wall of China like a huge snake lying asleep. At last our cars gained the final steep slope and passed through the narrow gateway in the Wall.

Before us lay Mongolia, a land of painted deserts dancing in mirage, of limitless grassy plains and nameless snow-capped mountains! Mongolia—a land of mystery and promise!

For 150 miles the trail led through grasslands. A band of several hundred robbers were somewhere near, and we had to travel with rifles in our hands. But they did not attack us. On the second day we came to the edge of the Gobi. The grass was short and stiff as wire. Clumps of low thorny bushes grew between the Gobi sage brush. It was a gravel desert, not sand like the Sahara.

Our geologists told us we were riding over sedimentary rocks. That was fine, but it did us no good unless we could find a place where the plain was cut by the bed

On the ridge above stretched the Great Wall of China.

of a stream or by tell-tale ravines and deep gullies.

We did not see that kind of a spot until the third day. In the late afternoon, the cars reached a bare, gravel bluff on the edge of a wide salt-marsh basin. The paleontologists wanted to stop to hunt for fossils. I said I would go on and make camp.

Our tents were pitched at the base of a gray-white ridge which looked to me like limestone. While I was watching a gorgeous sunset, the paleontologists' cars swung around a rock corner and roared into camp. I went out to meet them

Dr. Granger's eyes were shining, and Dr. Berkey was strangely silent. I knew something had happened. Silently Granger dug into his pockets and produced a handful of fossil bone fragments. Out of his shirt came other chunks. "These," he said, "are the first fossils ever found on the Mongolian plateau." We were so excited that we laughed and shouted and shook hands. We pounded each other on the back and did all the things men do when they are very happy.

While dinner was being prepared that evening, Dr. Granger wandered off along the ridge above the tents. Even in the fading light, he discovered a half-dozen bits of bone. Apparently there was another fossil deposit at our very door.

We were all so eager for the next day's work that the camp was astir shortly after daylight. Before breakfast I saw Dr. Berkey with head bent and hands behind his back, wandering about on the ridge. Soon he came in carrying a big fossil bone. One end was broken. Dr. Granger examined it with a puzzled expression.

"For the life of me," he said, "I cannot make that any-

The expedition always had to watch out for bandits.

thing except reptile. I wish we had the rest of it."

Ten minutes later his wish was granted. Dr. Black brought the missing part, which he had stepped on near his tent. It had rolled down from the ridge above. We were sure then that it was a reptile.

After breakfast the geologists went up to the spot where Dr. Berkey had found the bone. I was just about to set a line of traps for small mammals when Dr. Berkey hurried down to my tent. He seemed very excited but would tell me nothing. All he said was, "Come with me. We have made a very important discovery."

When we reached the crest of the ridge, I saw Dr. Granger on his knees with a whisk broom brushing sand away from something in the ground. "Take a look," Dr. Berkey said, "and tell me what you make of it."

I saw a great bone, beautifully preserved, lying in the rock. There was no doubt this time. It was reptilian and, moreover, *dinosaur*. I was breathless with excitement. "It means," Dr. Berkey said, "that we have discovered the *first rocks of the Age of Reptiles and the first dinosaur ever known from Asia north of the Himalaya Mountains!*"

We looked at it with awe, too impressed to speak for a while. Our gamble about finding fossils in Mongolia had paid off in a big way. This was a historic event. We had added a new chapter to the known geological history of the earth. That dinosaur bone was the first proof that we were correct in thinking that Asia is the place where much of the life of Europe and America began. We felt like prospectors who had gone into a new country hunting for gold when everybody said no gold was there. And then we struck a rich mine. For me it was much

The fossils were encased in a shell of burlap and plaster.

more important than to have found the richest gold mine in the world. Scientists are like that!

We were all so excited by the great discovery that everyone in camp wanted to hunt fossils. Even the Chinese cooks and the Mongols caught the fever. They were always out on the ridge looking for bones. I was supposed to be trapping small mammals, but I couldn't keep away from the fossil field. It was too fascinating.

On the second morning I started out alone. In my canvas bag was a whisk broom, a camel's-hair brush and several steel awls and chisels. I carried a small, light pickax, and a revolver hung in a holster at my waist.

A half mile from the tents I walked along the side of the gray-white outcrop. In the gravel were many fragments of fossil bone. Some were little pieces, only two or three inches long. I could see them easily, for they were gleaming white and looked quite different from the other stones. Once these had been large bones, but wind and frost had worn away the rock in which they were buried and had broken them up.

I knew that when so many fragments lay on the surface, there must be complete bones somewhere. Probably hundreds of skeletons lay just under the very earth on which I walked, but where? If only I had x-ray eyes and could see beneath the covering of sand and gravel! Of course, there was no use to dig unless I saw something to show that fossils were actually there. The only thing to do was to move along slowly, looking at every foot of ground. My one hope was to find the end of an unbroken bone projecting above the surface.

For more than an hour I walked over the ridge, exploring the sides of every gully where fossils might be exposed. At last my eyes caught the glint of a tiny piece of bone sticking out of the sand. It was not more than five inches long, but when I pushed it with my foot, it didn't move. I bent down and tried to pull it out. No use. The bone was solid in the rock.

I stretched out on the ground and brushed the sand away with a whisk broom. More of the bone appeared and another beside it. With a small steel awl I broke up the loose rock over a three-foot space and swept it clean. More bones showed up. I was excited, for this might be another important discovery. Hurrying back to camp, I asked Dr. Granger to come out with me. He brought his assistant and a bag of tools.

They set to work with whisk brooms, small brushes and chisels to remove the top covering. There, only a foot or two beneath the surface, was a great mass of bones. It was surely dinosaur! A new kind of dinosaur!

This became one of the greatest deposits that we discovered in all Mongolia. For a month the expedition worked in this one spot and even then did not take out all the fossils. The bones were piled on top of each other like jackstraws. Perhaps we would uncover the end of a leg bone, only to find that it ran under another bone, which must be removed before the first could be touched.

Our geologists made a study of the place and told us that 70 or 80 million years ago, in the Age of Reptiles, this area had been a great lake. The way the bones were jumbled together showed that they must have been swept into a backwater, or whirlpool. When the dino-

Fossil bones are sometimes found piled like jackstraws.

saurs died, their bodies were carried into this whirlpool and came to rest. Then the flesh dropped off, and the bones sank into the soft mud. After many, many years they were petrified, or changed to stone.

Along the shores of the lake, there must have been much vegetation. We know this because many of the bones were those of a Duckbill dinosaur which could eat only soft plants. It had a great, flattened mouth, just like the bill of a duck. He was a big fellow—thirty or forty feet long—and walked on his hind legs. His jaws had a great many small, weak teeth that could be used only for grinding up green stuff.

These large reptiles couldn't fight or protect them-

In dinosaur days most of the world was jungle and swamp.

selves from the fierce flesh-eating, or carnivorous (*car-niv'-or-ous*), dinosaurs that killed them for food. So when a flesh-eater attacked them, they tried to get into deep water. Sometimes in the battle both of them drowned. We are pretty sure this is what happened because the bones of flesh-eaters were all mixed up with the skeletons of Duckbills.

One day while the work of taking out the fossils went on, I sat on a ridge above the "quarry." And I thought of what this country must have been like 70 million years ago, back in the Age of Reptiles. The climate was warm and humid then. There was much rain. A thick jungle of palm and fig trees and other tropical plants rolled away in waves of green. Countless dinosaurs swarmed over the land and splashed in the waters of the lake.

Today that nightmare world is gone. Only wolves and white-tailed gazelles trot across the plains. Mongols, in yellow robes or gowns of flaming red, ride toward the white-walled temple in the basin. The edges of a bitter salt marsh mark the lake where water once lapped against the ridge upon which I sat.

Now there was no lush tropical vegetation. Instead, I could see only hummocks of sand, crowned with thorny plants. It was a desolate place, parched and blistering under the summer's sun. In the winter it was a frozen waste swept by icy gales from the Arctic Ocean.

But because the country was dry and wind-blown, we could find fossils. No grass or trees protected the soil from wind and weather. Gradually, bit by bit, the top surface had been worn away, exposing the bones that lay buried underneath. The softer rocks were cut into ravines and gullies giving a cross section of the ground many feet deep.

People speak of "digging for fossils," but as a rule very little digging is done. Sometimes a large specimen is found in the face of a bank. Then it may be necessary to scrape away the surface with a shovel to get down to the fossil itself. A dinosaur skeleton extends over a wide area. So a good deal of top soil must be taken off by scrapers and even dynamite. But that is only with the big fellows. In removing smaller specimens, a shovel is used very little. The surrounding rock is chipped away with small steel instruments. The sediment is brushed off with whisk brooms and camel's-hair brushes.

As the bone is exposed, it is soaked with shellac. This hardens all the loose particles. Then pieces of soft, tough Japanese rice paper are worked into all the crevices. These are saturated with shellac and allowed to dry.

Hunting Dinosaurs With a Whisk Broom

After one side of the fossil has been exposed, strips of burlap soaked in flour paste are laid on. When this is dry, it forms a hard shell. Then the bone is turned over and bandaged on the other side.

When the fossils reach the museum, the burlap cover is softened with water and stripped off. The bone is there, just as it was removed in the field.

Fossil hunting is not all excitement. Sometimes a man will walk a whole day and find nothing at all or only chips of bone. Usually the weather is hot. The sun beats down unmercifully in that dry area. The scientist climbs up and down the face of cliffs or the sides of ravines. He is tired and thirsty, but he keeps at the job. Per-

Dr. Granger used field glasses to hunt signs of fossils.

haps in the next few yards he may discover a great treasure.

An expert collector has trained eyes. He can recognize the difference between fossil bone and ordinary rock when a long way off. Something in the color or shape gives the clew.

At one place in the Gobi Desert, Dr. Granger developed a new way to find fossils. The land was cut by hundreds of narrow ravines parallel to each other. He would sit on a ridge and with powerful field glasses examine every foot of the opposite slope. The fossils in that deposit were pure white. They showed plainly to his practiced eyes.

The Red Deer River of Alberta, Canada, was a wonderful place for dinosaurs. One scientist floated down the river on a houseboat, watching the shore on either side. When a spot looked promising, he landed and climbed up the bank. In India this same man used elephants to carry him over the fossil fields. In Greece he used donkeys, in Egypt camels. But as a rule one's own legs make the best transport for fossil hunting.

THUNDER LIZARD
AND KING OF TYRANTS

First, there are a few facts that must be explained. The earth is about two billion years old. That great period of time has been divided into eras by scientists. The Age of Reptiles is called the Mesozoic (*Mes-o-zo'-ic*), or Middle Era. Each era is further divided into periods. The Mesozoic Era has three periods: Triassic (*Tri-ass'-ic*), Jurassic (*Ju-rass'-ic*), and Cretaceous (*Kree-ta'-shus*).

Triassic, the oldest, began about 200 million years ago.

All About Dinosaurs

That is when the first dinosaurs appeared. Cretaceous, the youngest, ended 60 million years ago. Thus during 140 million years reptiles ruled the world: dinosaurs on land, marine reptiles in the ocean, and flying reptiles in the air.

There are no simple, everyday names for dinosaurs, so we must use the scientific names. Every name is put together out of Latin or Greek words, and they are supposed to indicate something about the animal. For instance, the name of the greatest of all flesh-eating dinosaurs is *Tyrannosaurus rex*. This comes from *Tyranno* (tyrant) *sauros* (lizard) *rex* (king). Thus it means "King of the tyrant lizards."

Brontosaurus, The Thunder Lizard

Best known to the public of all the dinosaurs is the great Brontosaurus (*Bron'-toe-sawr'-us*). The man who gave the animal its name said it was so big the earth must have thundered when it walked, but anyway it was a "thundering big reptile." This is the dinosaur pictured most often in the "funnies." It figured in a movie called "The Lost World." Cartoonists often show it chasing terrified explorers through a strange jungle of prehistoric plants. Of course, that is all imagination. The dino-

Tyrannosaurus was the greatest
of all flesh-eating dinosaurs.

saur lived in the Jurassic period 100 million years ago, and no men were alive then.

The Thunder Lizard was 60 to 70 feet in length—almost twice as long as an ordinary schoolroom. Probably it weighed about 80,000 pounds. That is more than ten elephants! The very long neck and tail made up a good deal of the length of the animal, but the head was so small that it must have looked utterly ridiculous.

The small brain weighed less than a pound. It shows that the creature was just about as stupid as an animal could be and still live. Probably all its actions were directed by instinct, and very little by conscious intelligence. The mouth was so small, and the spoon-shaped teeth so weak, that the Thunder Lizards must have had to eat continually. Otherwise, the great hulking mass of flesh and bones never could have stayed alive.

Brontosaurus spent its life wading about in the shallows of lakes and rivers, and in swamps. With its long neck it could easily reach the plants that formed its food. The water helped to support its huge body, too. Although the legs looked like tree trunks, and were very heavy, the joints were poorly formed.

This shows that the creature spent very little time on land. It had to come out at some time to lay eggs, but it

Brachiosaurus was even heavier than the Thunder Lizard.

couldn't go far from the water. It wouldn't dare to do so anyway, for it might be killed and eaten by the fierce carnivorous dinosaurs that roamed all over the country.

In spite of its size, Brontosaurus had no means of defense. So, when it saw a flesh-eater prowling on shore, snapping its great bear-trap jaws, the Thunder Lizard pushed out into deep water where the attacker could not follow.

The Thunder Lizard and the King of Tyrants

During the Jurassic period when Brontosaurus lived, Wyoming, Montana and other of our western states were occupied by shallow lakes and rivers. The Rocky Mountains had not yet been born. Today that country is made up of bare, grassy plains with few trees. Then it was covered with wonderful vegetation. Many dinosaurs lived and died there. It is the best place for hunting fossils in the entire world.

Dr. Walter Granger, who later was with me in the Gobi Desert, spent many years collecting fossils in Wyoming. In 1898, near Medicine Bow, Wyoming, he discovered a Brontosaurus skeleton. With two men he worked six months taking out the bones. The museum people spent four years in piecing together the broken parts and mounting the skeleton. The petrified bones were very heavy. One upper leg bone alone weighed 570 pounds. When the skeleton was mounted, it measured 66 feet 8 inches in length, and 15 feet 2 inches in height. Those of you who live in New York City must have seen the Brontosaurus in the American Museum of Natural History. If not you had better go, for you will never forget it.

Brontosaurus was a member of the group of dinosaurs known as the Sauropoda (*So-rop'-o-da*). They were the

All About Dinosaurs

largest animals that ever walked on four legs. Another was called Diplodocus (*Di-plod'-o-kus*). It was more slender than its cousin. It was the longest of all dinosaurs because of its extraordinary whip-like tail. The nostrils, or nose openings, were placed on the top of the head so that it could breathe while its body was under water.

The finest skeletons of Diplodocus are in the Carnegie Museum in Pittsburgh, Pennsylvania.

Brachiosaurus (*Brake'-e-o-sawr'-us*) was even heavier than the Thunder Lizard. Its nostrils were raised on a sort of hump on the very summit of the head. Thus the great dinosaur could wade on the bottom feeding on the soft vegetation. Sometimes it would poke its head above

Brachiosaurus had nostrils on the top of his head.

This giant meat-eater is called Allosaurus.

the surface and look about, just as men in a submarine use the periscope to observe the scene above water.

Allosaurus

The principal enemy of the Thunder Lizard was Allosaurus (*Al'-lo-sawr'-us*). He was the mighty hunter of the Jurassic period. He was 35 feet long and stalked across the country in majestic splendor. Like the lion or tiger of today, he was lord of all he surveyed. Allosaurus was a giant meat-eater. When you look at his enormous jaws armed with dagger-like teeth, you can understand why all other dinosaurs were terrified when he appeared.

Allosaurus walked only on his hind legs. He could

A mounted skeleton of Allosaurus devouring Brontosaurus.

leap and strike with great quickness. The heavy tail balanced his body, for his front legs were very small and he seldom came down on all fours. His hands ended in great hooked claws which were regular talons. They helped him hold his prey and tear the flesh off the bones.

We have proof that Allosaurus killed and ate the big Thunder Lizards. A skeleton of Brontosaurus, found in Wyoming, had parts of the backbone bitten off, and tooth marks showed on many of the bones. When the Allosaurus jaw was compared with these marks, it fitted them exactly. Also broken teeth of Allosaurus were mixed with the Brontosaurus bones. In the same deposit of fossils, the remains of other vegetable-feeding dinosaurs showed they had been scraped by the teeth of the big flesh-eater.

The skeleton of an Allosaurus is mounted in the American Museum of Natural History as though the animal were feeding on a dead Thunder Lizard.

Tyrannosaurus rex

Imagine the shore of a lagoon near the great inland sea of Montana. Then pretend it is 70 million years ago in the Cretaceous period, long after Allosaurus lived.

It is a low-lying country, broken by thick clumps of ginkgo and sycamore trees. There are many figs, palms and bananas, too. The day is hot. Banks of mist hang over the water.

A huge vegetable-feeding dinosaur Trachodon (*Track'-o-don*) waddles along the shore, pushing its broad duck-like bill into the mud. It finds soft bulbs and trailing water plants—food it loves. Suddenly it hears a sound. Swinging about, it sees the gigantic figure of

All About Dinosaurs

a Tyrannosaurus (*Tie-ran'-o-sawr'-us*) dimly outlined among the trees of the forest's edge. The ugly head towers among the highest branches. The ponderous tail stretches backward, lost in smothering vegetation.

Wild with fear, the Trachodon hurries toward the water. But its fat, hulking body can only move slowly. In two leaps, the King of Tyrants lands on its back. The giant's head seems to split apart as the great mouth opens and clamps shut on the Duckbill's neck. The dagger-teeth crunch through bones and flesh like shears cutting paper. There is frantic thrashing for a time as the colossal beasts roll in the slippery muck. Then the Trachodon lies still. Its head hangs loosely, almost severed from the neck by six-inch teeth.

Tyrannosaurus rex, the King of Tyrants, rises on its two powerful hind legs and looks about. The fifty-foot body is balanced by a heavy tail. Its head is massive and the jaws four feet long. The short forelimbs seem tiny, but the clawed hands have a grip of iron. Nothing about Tyrannosaurus is weak. It is the most terrible creature of destruction that ever walked upon the earth!

For a few moments, the Tyrant King gazes into the dark reaches of the jungle and out across the water. Then it settles to the feast. Huge chunks of warm flesh, torn

The great mouth clamps shut on the Duckbill's neck.

from the Duckbill's body, slide down the cave-like throat. At the end of an hour, half the skeleton lies naked. The King's stomach is full to bursting. Walking slowly to the jungle, he stretches out beneath a palm tree. For days, or perhaps a week, he lies motionless in a death-like sleep. When his stomach is empty, he gets to his feet and goes out to kill again. That is his life—killing, eating and sleeping.

Duckbills were not the Tyrant's only prey. Any of the smaller dinosaurs might die under the weight of its great body and crushing jaws. Thanks to Dr. Barnum Brown of the American Museum of Natural History, we know much of Tyrannosaurus and his habits. In 1900 Dr. Brown found part of a skeleton in South Dakota. More bones of a different creature were unearthed two years later on Hell Creek, Montana. That was half a century ago, and Montana was still the Wild West.

Dr. Brown said his base of supplies was at Miles City on the railroad. This was 130 miles from the Bad Lands where he had heard he might find dinosaur fossils. For five days he and his men marched across rolling prairie and at last reached the little log post office of Jordan, Montana. Ten miles farther they entered the Bad Lands, a wilderness of cliffs and domes, cut by canyons, ravines and gullies. The rocks looked as though they had been painted in brilliant colors of red, yellow and orange. The country was good for fossil hunting but little else. That is why it was called Bad Lands.

Dr. Brown made camp on Hell Creek. Nearby the stream had cut into a hill, exposing rounded sandstones which had rolled down to the water. Some of them contained bones, and the fossil hunters traced them to their

A complete skeleton of Tyrannosaurus was hauled out.

source halfway up the hill. There, in a layer of buff-colored sand, they found the first complete skeleton of Tyrannosaurus. Most of it lay just as the animal died, seventy million years ago. The bones were petrified and enclosed in a bluish sandstone almost as hard as granite.

The loose surface could be easily removed, but lower down the rock was like iron. In order to get to the bone level, slices of the hillside had to be carved off with plows, scrapers and even dynamite. Finally, the men made a hole in the hill 30 feet long, 20 feet wide and 25 feet deep.

For two summers they worked at the job of taking out the skeleton. Some of the sandstone blocks containing bones were of huge size. One weighed 4,150 pounds, and four horses were needed to drag it in a wagon across the plains to the railroad.

In 1908 Dr. Brown found another skeleton in the same Montana Bad Lands. All three skeletons stand among the most prized exhibits in the American Museum. Every year millions of people gaze at the petrified bones of the King of Tyrants.

THE DUCKBILL DINOSAURS

Although you were introduced to Trachodon in the last chapter, there is much more to be said about him. For one thing, we know exactly what his skin was like because we have a Duckbill "mummy." Actually it is a dried-up dinosaur, 60 or 70 million years old! This is possibly the most extraordinary fossil ever discovered. I'll tell you about it in a moment. First, let's take a look at the animal itself.

Trachodon was 30 feet long and stood 16 feet high.

The Duckbill Dinosaurs

He was shaped somewhat like a kangaroo, with short arms, long hind legs and a wide thick tail. Most of the time he walked on his hind feet. He might get down on all fours when he was feeding. His front limbs helped him to push himself into an upright position, but they weren't of much account as real legs. The hind feet had three well-developed toes ending in broad hoofs. The fingers of the small hands were connected by skin to form paddles like a duck's foot. With these paddles and the heavy flattened tail, Trachodon must have been a good swimmer and spent much time in the water.

But the most peculiar thing about this dinosaur is its head. The front part was expanded to form a broad duckbill, and must have been covered with a horny sheath. It is quite plain that with such a mouth, Trachodon could eat little except vegetable food. Also the teeth show that he fed on soft plants. He had no teeth in the front of his bill, but on each side of both jaws 500 teeth are arranged in rows. One row is piled on top of the other. Two thousand teeth altogether! What an opportunity for a toothache! As soon as one tooth wore out, another pushed up from underneath to take its place.

Duckbills lived at the end of the Cretaceous period. Then the climate of the northern part of North America was much warmer than it is today. It was about like southern California. The impressions of thousands of plants and leaves show that palms, resembling the palmetto of Florida, fig trees, ginkgos, and even redwoods made up a luxuriant forest. But most abundant of all were horsetail rushes. Probably Trachodon ate quantities of those plants.

Everything about the animal indicates that it lived mostly in the water. It was probably the best swimmer of all dinosaurs. Although not related, it can be compared to the living South American iguanas. These reptiles exist today in great numbers on the Galápagos Islands, off the coast of Chile. They go far out in the ocean and feed entirely on seaweed, which grows on the bottom at some distance from shore. The iguana swims with a snake-like movement of its body and long sweeps of the tail. Its legs are pressed closely to its sides and remain motionless. Crocodiles do likewise. Probably that is the way Trachodon moved in the water.

In spite of their size, the Duckbills had no protection against flesh-eaters except their ability to swim. Thus they seldom ventured far from water. They did have to come out on land to lay their eggs. Also they liked to nuzzle through the mud with their flat bills possibly to vary their diet with fresh-water clams. But they always

Parasaurolophus had an air storage chamber in his crest.

had to be on watch for the King of Tyrants. One might jump out from the jungle at any moment. Then there would be a wild scramble as the Duckbills dashed for the water like frightened sea elephants, with the big flesh-eater leaping in pursuit.

Most of our large living animals, such as the elephant, rhinoceros and hippopotamus, have very thick skins, which give them some protection. They are called pachyderms (*pack'-e-derms*). Scientists at first thought that

Trachodon had a scaly skin and made guesses about it.

In 1908, the matter was settled definitely when Charles H. Sternberg of Kansas found a Duckbill mummy. This dinosaur died a natural death, for it shows no injuries. The body lay undisturbed for a long time, perhaps upon a broad sand flat in a stream at low water stage. The hot sun dried up the muscles and soft insides. The skin shrank around the legs and became hard and leathery. Over the stomach, the skin sank down into the body cavity and lay in creases and folds along the reptile's sides as the flesh dried up.

After this, the dried carcass was rapidly buried in fine river sand. Fortunately the sand contained enough clay to take a perfect impression of all the markings before the skin had time to soften in water. With a magnifying glass you can see every detail of the skin as it once existed even though the skin itself has disappeared.

The mummy shows that Trachodon was not covered with scales or any kind of protective armor. Instead the skin seems to have been "pebbled" like a golf ball. Moreover, it was quite thin. There is no certain way of knowing the color of the dinosaur, except that it was darker on the back and lighter underneath.

Trachodons were the most abundant of the large dinosaurs if one can judge by the number of skeletons that have been discovered. They are closely related to the Iguanodon, found in England in 1822 by Dr. Gideon Mantell. That was the first dinosaur ever to be described.

Later, seventeen Iguanodon skeletons were found in a coal mine at Bernissart, Belgium. They are among the historic discoveries of fossils and are mounted in the museum at Brussels.

During the long years of the Cretaceous period, a swift river cut its way through the coal-bearing rocks at Bernissart. The canyon was 750 feet deep, almost twice as great as the deepest part of the Gorge of Niagara. Then conditions changed, and the canyon began to fill with sediment. The stream became slow moving with marshy banks. There among luxuriant vegetation the Iguanodons lived and died. Their skeletons were buried and turned to stone. For 70 million years they lay undisturbed until a coal miner discovered their tomb.

Strangely enough, the first dinosaur to be described in America was also a Cretaceous relative of Iguanodon. It was found in Haddonfield, New Jersey, a suburb of Philadelphia. Workmen dug up the bones in a marl bed and distributed them around the neighborhood as curiosities. Eventually Mr. A. Parker Foulke reopened the diggings and unearthed more of the skeleton. Then he went on a hunt to find the bones that remained in various homes or were being used as doorstops. He recovered most of them, and the skeleton was studied by Professor Joseph Leidy. It was named Hadrosaurus (*Had'-ro-sawr'-us*). The reptile was 25 feet long and stood 12 feet high. But its brain weighed less than a pound. It was smaller than a man's clenched fist.

Trachodon had a good many other relatives. Some of them were extraordinary looking creatures with peculiar heads. Dr. Barnum Brown discovered several in the Red Deer River region of Alberta, Canada. One is a crested

Dinosaur bones were used as doorstops in Haddonfield.

dinosaur named Saurolophus (*Sawr'-o-loaf'-us*). It was imbedded in sandstone which showed wave marks and the impressions of horsetail rushes. Apparently the skeleton, with pieces of skin clinging to it, was buried on a sandy beach.

Millions of years passed, and the bones turned to stone. Hundreds of feet of earth piled upon them as the low-lying marshes filled with sediment. Finally the Red Deer River formed. It was a young water course and cut through these sediments to make a deep canyon. Millions of years later Dr. Brown saw the dinosaur bones sticking out of the rocks in the side of the river gorge 500 feet below the plain level.

On the back of the dinosaur's head was a great bony crest. In life this supported a leathery lobe of skin like that on the heads of some living lizards. *Saurolophus* was a big dinosaur. He was 32 feet long and stood 17 feet high. Like Trachodon he was a plant eater. There must have been a great many of them. In a single quarry bones of several hundred individuals had washed out on the bank.

Dr. Brown found another new dinosaur with a big crest in the Red Deer River Gorge. It was a first cousin of Trachodon. It was named Corythosaurus (*Kor-ith'-o-sawr'-us*). This means "Corinthian helmeted reptile."

Like the Trachodon mummy, this dinosaur had preserved much of the skin impressions and even some of the
tendons. Evidently the body had floated along a stream
and was caught in a backwater. There it lay stranded on
its left side. Unio clam shells were scattered about, and a
turtle lay above the tail. This fellow was 18 feet long and
was a swimming dinosaur. It, too, had a high bony ridge
on the top of its head.

Lambeosaurus (*Lam'-be-o-sawr'-us*), closely related
to Trachodon, had a crest divided at the top into two
hatchet-like blades. Parasaurolophus (*Par-a-sawr-o-loaf'-
us*) went even further. Its crest was very long and ex-
tended up and back over its head like a plume. The crest
was used as an air-storage chamber. Thus the dinosaur could remain for some time under water without
breathing.

Corythosaurus

was a swimming dinosaur.

ARMORED DINOSAURS

Not even the largest vegetable-feeding dinosaurs had any protection against the big flesh-eaters except to escape into deep water. But nature did something about that. Gradually some of the dinosaurs that lived entirely on land, clothed themselves in armor like knights of the Middle Ages.

The most fantastic of them all was the Jurassic Stegosaurus (*Steg'-o-sawr'-us*). He was a large reptile, 15 feet or more in length, with a small low-hung head. Four stout legs, ending in padded feet, supported his massive body. But the front limbs were so much shorter than the others that he seemed to be humped up behind.

The armor consisted of a series of upright, triangular, bony plates running down the middle of the back from head to tail. Some of these sharp-edged plates were two feet in height and not more than an inch thick. During life they were probably much longer and covered with horn. The tip of the 10-foot tail carried four huge spikes, 3 feet long and 6 inches thick at the base. When the dino-

This dinosaur with a spiked frill is called Styracosaurus.

saur swung this weapon from side to side, it could rip open the belly of a hungry meat-eating dinosaur.

This dinosaur is famous, also, because of its tiny brain. Although the body was bigger than an elephant, the absurdly small head contained a brain no larger than a walnut! In the hips, an enlargement of the spinal cord was 20 times the size of the brain. This nerve center controlled the movements of the heavy hind limbs and the powerful tail. It has given rise to the idea that Stegosaurus had two brains—one in its head and one in the tail. This, of course, is not true, but certainly the dinosaur must have been even more stupid than the huge Thunder Lizard.

Ankylosaurus

This completely armored dinosaur lived 70 or 80 million years ago in the Cretaceous period. It had a low squat body. This was protected by heavy bone plates even on the head, and a thick, stiff tail ending in a huge club-like mass of bone that could deal a crushing blow. There you have Ankylosaurus (*An-kyle'-o-sawr'-us*). He could blunder along, minding his own business, confident that even the giant King of Tyrants would leave him severely alone. If some hungry flesh-eater was foolish enough to think it could find a meal in Ankylosaurus, this armored dinosaur had only to swing that mighty tail club. The flesh-eaters soon discovered that attacking him wasn't good enough.

A Cretaceous relative, Palaeoscincus (*Pale-e-o-skink'-us*), lived the same kind of life. He resembled a giant armadillo. He was armored from head to tail with a row of huge projecting spikes along the lower sides of his body. Heaven help the reptile that tried to attack Palaeoscincus!

Triceratops

Of all the armored dinosaurs, Triceratops (*Tri-cer'-a-tops*) is the most interesting and spectacular. He belongs to the group known as Ceratopsia (*Cer-a-top'-si-a*). Of course, you know what an army tank looks like. Well, if Triceratops were alive, and standing at a distance in the grass, you might think he was a tank. You would see a thick, squat body, 30 feet long, and an enormous head ending in a great flared shield. From its center, two "guns" point forward. But as you come closer, what appear to be the muzzles of machine guns, turn out to be a pair of long horns. On the nose, above the hooked, parrot-like beak, stands the third upright horn, shorter than the

Paleoscincus was armored from head to tail.

others. The three horns give it the name Triceratops. If you looked Triceratops squarely in the face, you would notice a thick guard of overhanging bone in front of each eye.

This dinosaur was a terrible fighting machine. None could stand against him except the King of Tyrants. I doubt if even that creature of destruction often attacked a Triceratops. We know battles did occur, because we have found broken horns that had partly repaired themselves. Probably these combats were mostly among the Triceratops themselves, in jealousy over some lady friend. I would like to have seen such a struggle. Two ten-ton bodies launching themselves at each other, charging horn against horn, shield against shield!

When you look at a skeleton of Triceratops, you are impressed by the size of the skull. It is nearly one-third the length of the body. That is because it covers huge neck muscles attached to the shield. With these muscles and very strong leg muscles, Triceratops could make a powerful up-thrust with its horns.

Several other dinosaurs from this group have neck shields and horns of various shapes. I'll just mention their names. One was Styracosaurus (*Sty-rack'-o-sawr'-us*). He had a large horn on the nose, only short ones above the eyes, and spikes along the edge of the "frill," or shield.

Then there was Chasmosaurus (*Kas'-mo-sawr'-us*) with very small horns and an upstanding shield. Also Monoclonius (*Mon-o-klon'-e-us*). He bore one large horn on the nose, like a rhinoceros, and short thick projections over the eyes.

All of the Ceratopsians were land, vegetable-eating reptiles. They lived along the marshes of the great inland

Triceratops had a body 30 feet long and an enormous head.

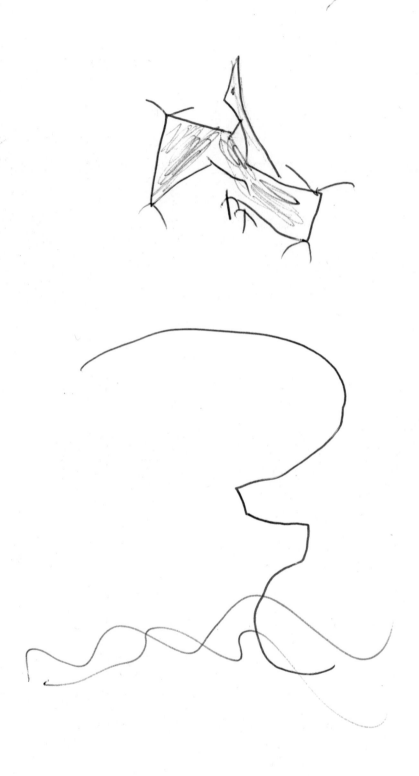

seas east of the Rocky Mountains. It was a pleasant home. A sub-tropical climate nourished fig and palm trees, red-woods, and ginkgos. Grass grew knee-high. The big horned reptiles could browse peacefully, only keeping one eye open for a prowling Tryannosaurus.

The Ceratopsia were the last of the dinosaurs. They entered the scene late in dinosaur evolution, and no one knew where they came from.

Monoclonius had a great horn on his nose like a rhinoceros.

DINOSAURS
OF THE FLAMING CLIFFS

I have told how our Central Asiatic Expedition discovered the first dinosaurs known from Asia. That happened as soon as we got into the Gobi Desert. That was a good beginning, and luck continued. New mammals, plants and fossil animals were found almost every day.

There was excitement of other kinds, too. Sometimes we sat huddled in the tents for hours while sandstorms raged. Bandits were reported in the grasslands to the north of us. Their leader was a giant Mongol named

Kula. He was reported to be a terrible man. When he attacked a caravan, he murdered every man, woman and child. We feared he might try to get our motor cars if he heard of our expedition. That would have meant a battle.

But week after week we plunged deeper into the Gobi. At last we were too far out in the waterless desert for Kula to follow. Only camels could live there. Kula's horses would have died of thirst and starvation.

But the weather was getting colder. Golden plover drifted down from the Arctic tundras in great flocks. Geese and ducks formed black lines against the sky. Sometimes light snow powdered the desert. Those were signs of winter that no explorer could ignore. The main caravan trail was many miles away through unexplored country. If we were caught by a blizzard, we might never be able to get out. I was worried.

When we started home, our navigators had set a course by compass straight across the desert. The going was very bad for the cars. We had to drive over gravel and sand and wind-blown hummocks covered with thorny bushes. For 100 miles there had been no sign of water. Our water bags were dry, and we were thirsty because every drop had to go into the cars. An hour before sunset on the third day, I saw a Mongol tent, or *yurt*, far away. Where there were people there must be water!

Our photographer, J. B. Shackleford, was with me in the leading car far in front of the fleet. I said to him, "You wait here and stop the others when they come. I'll go to the yurt and ask where we can find water."

He got out, and I drove to the Mongol camp. Only a man and his wife were there. He told me of a well not far away.

When I returned to the cars, all the men were gathered about Dr. Walter Granger, the chief paleontologist. In his hand he held a white skull, 8 inches long.

"Take a look at this," he said. "What do you think of it?"

I examined it carefully. It was a reptile and probably dinosaur, but I had never seen anything like it.

"Where," I asked, "did you get it?"

"Shackleford found it just over there," Granger said.

He pointed to the north where the top of a red cliff showed above the rim of the plain. Shack said he had told the men in the other cars to wait for me, and then he had wandered off toward the red cliff. There he stood on the edge of a great badland depression. He walked down into it a little way to see what it was like. Right in front of

Shackelford found a white skull at the base of the cliff.

him, resting on a piece of red sandstone, was the white skull. He picked it up and hurried back to the cars. Shack's discovery was so exciting that we knew we had to search further.

The Mongol had told me of a well in the depression which we call a "basin." This was the spot for us. We agreed to camp overnight near the well. "Then we can hunt fossils till dark," I said.

You can't imagine what a beautiful place it was. We

looked into a vast pink bowl. It had been scooped out of the plain by the action of wind and frost and rain. In the basin giant hills stood alone like strange living beasts carved from sandstone. One of them we named the "dinosaur" for it resembled a Brontosaurus sitting on its haunches. Other formations looked like castles of the Middle Ages. We could imagine spires and towers, gateways, walls and ramparts.

Caves ran deep into the rock, cut by ravines and gullies. At the beginning of darkness, a wild, mysterious beauty lay with the purple shadows in every canyon. In the last rays of the setting sun, the rocks seemed to be on fire. We named the place "The Flaming Cliffs."

The day was September 2, 1922. As soon as camp was made, all of us scattered over the basin floor looking for fossils. Bits of white bone were everywhere. Several men saw skeletons partly exposed in the rock. There wasn't time to take them out, for night was on us.

In the morning it was hard to leave such a wonderful place, but the feel of snow was in the air! We might be trapped if we waited even one day more, so we pushed ahead. Two days later the blizzard came. By then we had reached the main caravan trail and were safe, but it was a narrow escape.

As soon as we returned to our house in Peking, one of the men left for New York. He carried with him the small white reptile skull Shackleford had discovered at the Flaming Cliffs. A month later we had a cable from Professor Osborn, President of the American Museum of Natural History. "You have made a very important discovery. The reptile is the long-sought ancestor of Triceratops. It has been named Protoceratops andrewsi (*Pro-toe-cer'-a-tops an-drew'-si*) in your honor. Go back and get more."

The next summer we did go back to the Flaming Cliffs. We went through the desolation of a sun-parched desert. For ten months there had been no rain. We followed the tracks our motor cars had made ten months before. Even the hard, wire-like grass lay brown and dead in the burning sun. White rims of alkali marked the beds of former ponds. The desert swam in a maddening, dancing mirage. Reedy lakes and cool, forested islands were mirrored where we knew there was only sand.

We traveled mile after mile without seeing a living thing except spotted lizards and long-tailed gazelles that do not need water. The way was marked by the skulls of camels and of sheep. Beside the dead ashes of a camp fire, lay the skeleton of a Mongol woman. Her bones had

The leader of the camel caravan agreed to bring supplies.

been picked clean by wolves and vultures. The few Mongols who used to live there had all moved away because they could find no water.

Before we started, I told Merin, the leader of our caravan, that he must cross this desolate place. His camels were to carry the gasoline and supplies that would make it possible for the expedition to work. He said, "I can not go. The camels will die."

"That is true, but some will live," I told him. "Leave the weak ones behind, but bring twenty camels with gasoline and food. I'll make up twenty special loads."

He shook his head, for he was an old-time caravan

leader. He did not want to lose the camels even though they belonged to me. To him it was a point of honor to bring all his camels through alive and well.

Finally Merin agreed to try. "I will come," he said at last. That was enough. I knew he would keep his word and that I could count on him to bring us the supplies to carry on.

Our motor cars carried us a hundred miles a day over the forsaken waste. In midsummer we again pitched our tents at the well of the Flaming Cliffs. We arrived at three o'clock in the afternoon. Before night every fossil hunter had found a skeleton. Even I had a share in the finds. While walking in the bottom of a ravine, I saw a pipe lying beside a rock. It was one that Dr. Granger had lost the year before. Strangely enough, it had dropped within a few inches of the skull and jaws of a Protoceratops andrewsi.

For more than a month we worked at this one spot. Seventy-five skulls and twelve skeletons of Protoceratops were taken out. They showed every stage in the growth of this ancestral dinosaur.

Nothing like this series has ever been discovered. They begin with a newly hatched baby only a few inches long. This little fellow had no shield, or "frill." As the dinosaur grew, the shield must have grown also. It got bigger and bigger, and in the very old individuals covered the entire neck. That is like the shield of the giant Triceratops. The front of the face of Protoceratops formed a hooked, parrot-like beak. But although he is the ancestor of the horned dinosaurs, he had no horns. This is not surprising, for he was the first of his line. The horns had not yet begun to develop.

I must admit that even though Protoceratops andrewsi was named for me, he was one of the ugliest of all the small dinosaurs. His short, toad-like body seemed to be mostly head. A piece of bone from the frill projected downward on each side of his face. It looked like a long wart. His short legs were badly bowed. The tail was fat and thick. He crawled on his belly. No leaping or running for him. For food, he probably nipped off bits of the desert plants with his hooked beak. No, I can't be proud of his looks. But this dinosaur helped scientists to understand where the Ceratopsians originated, and how they came to look the way they did.

Even after five weeks at the Flaming Cliffs, we were still finding fossils. Each one seemed finer than the last. One beautiful skeleton was lying on its belly. The head and neck were stretched out and the legs drawn up as if

Mosasaurs and plesiosaurs battled in the Kansas Inland Sea.

it were about to crawl forward. The dinosaur lay exactly as it died 70 million years ago. The fine red sand had drifted gently over the body before the flesh dropped away. Every bone was in place, even to the end of the tail. Tendons along the back showed plainly. Where the stomach had been, there were a dozen rounded pebbles. The dinosaur must have swallowed them to help grind up its food as a chicken swallows gravel.

Although most of the fossils were Protoceratops, two or three kinds of small, flesh-eating dinosaurs were discovered. We also found parts of a crocodile. That shows there must have been a stream or small lake in the basin at some time. The geologists are sure, however, that when Protoceratops lived there, the climate was dry. It was a semi-desert.

While we were reaping this wonderful harvest of fossils, my mind was not at rest. As leader of the expedition, I was responsible for the health and safety of the men, as well as for the work. Food was very low. Only enough gasoline remained for one car. Merin had not arrived with our supplies.

I sent out our Mongols on horseback to see if they could find our camels. They returned with no word. Day after day we scanned the horizon. Always disappointment. Hundreds of gazelles lived on the plains north of the Flaming Cliffs. From horseback, I could kill three or four almost any day. So we had meat in plenty, but little else to eat.

At last only two sacks of flour remained. We needed flour to make paste for removing fossils. When that was gone, work must stop. I asked the men what we should do. For food, the flour would last only a few days. For paste, it would be enough to take out many bones. Everyone voted to use the flour for work. "After all," they said, "that is more important than food. We won't starve, for there are always gazelles." I was sure that would be their decision. Fossils are much more important to a paleontologist than food!

At the end of five weeks, one of Merin's Mongols rode into camp. The caravan was safe, and only sixty miles away. Many of the camels had died, but thirty had come through with food and gasoline. It was a happy day for us when we saw the big white lead camel stalking across the desert carrying an American flag. The animals were weak and thin, with flapping humps and flat bellies, but with rest and food they would soon recover. They had brought enough food and supplies for us to continue our work.

The big white lead camel carried an American flag.

Only a hundred miles from the Flaming Cliffs, we discovered another wonderful place. This we called the "Oshi Basin." I saw it first when standing at the top of a mountain. As far as my eyes could see in any direction, the country was unexplored. Off to the north, a strange red plateau crowned with black, glowed in the sunlight. This was something new and different!

We went to it through a rocky gateway between high

Off to the north, we saw a strange red plateau.

All About Dinosaurs

cliffs. There, in the very center of a long valley stood a
blood-red plateau. It was covered with black lava, like
the chocolate frosting on a giant's cake. A stone wall shut
off the entrance to the valley. That had been made by
human hands thousands of years before Mongols came
into the country.

At the far end, the valley broke off into a wild maze of
ravines and gullies. We camped on the very edge of a
deep canyon. In the evening shadows, the rocks took on
fantastic shapes. We seemed to be living in the world of
a long-gone yesterday. At any moment, I imagined that
dinosaurs might wander to the doorways of our tents
from out of the gloomy chasms!

Dinosaurs had been there more than a 100 million
years ago in the Upper Jurassic period. That we knew
because we found their bones. They were of the Sauropoda, the giant dinosaurs, like Brontosaurus. These reptiles usually lived along the marshy shores of lakes. Therefore this valley must have had water at one time with a
warm, tropical climate and lush vegetation. There were
not many bones, but enough to tell us that those dinosaurs
were larger even than Brontosaurus or Diplodocus.

In this valley Dr. Granger found a ledge of pure iron.
In it lay the skeleton of a small dinosaur. The bones had

become iron also. He tried to take it out, but the metal blunted his steel implements. At last he decided to leave it. Enough of the skeleton was exposed to show that it belonged to a new family of dinosaurs. All he could do was to make drawings of what was there.

Another small dinosaur proved to be of great importance. It was only a little fellow. Professor Osborn named it Psittacosaurus (*Sit'-a-ko-sawr'-us*). Its chief characteristic was the very deep, pointed beak like a parrot. Other features of the skeleton showed that it probably was the direct ancestor of Protoceratops and thus of all Ceratopsian dinosaurs.

Perhaps you wonder why I have written so much about these little dinosaurs. Even though they were small, they showed that the group of Ceratopsians started in Mongolia and Central Asia. After millions of years they began to wander. They went northwest to Siberia and across the land bridge that connected Asia and America at the Bering Straits. All the time they were getting bigger. When they had spread over northern America, they reached their greatest size in Triceratops. It was then, at the end of the Cretaceous period, that they, and all other dinosaurs, disappeared from the face of the earth.

DINOSAUR EGG HUNTING

Until we went to the Gobi Desert, no one knew how dinosaurs produced their young. It was supposed that they laid eggs because dinosaurs were reptiles and most reptiles lay eggs. Still, no dinosaur eggs had been found anywhere in the world. But on the second day at the Flaming Cliffs, George Olsen came in for luncheon with a strange story. He said he had discovered some fossil eggs. All of us joked him about it at first. We thought they would prove to be stones shaped like eggs. "Laugh if you want to," he said, "but they are eggs all right. Come with me."

We had to walk only a short distance from camp. Olsen pointed to a small rock ledge. There lay three eggs, eight inches long. Dr. Granger picked one up, and all of us gathered around him. The egg was heavy, for the inside was solid red sandstone. The shell was broken, but it looked just like regular eggshell only thicker. It was brown and completely petrified.

Dr. Granger finally said, "Gentlemen, there is no doubt about it. You are looking at the first dinosaur egg ever found." Maybe you think we weren't excited!

But then we thought, could these be anything except dinosaur eggs? They were about eight inches long and bluntly pointed at both ends. Birds' eggs have one end pointed and the other round, so they won't roll out of the nest. Most reptile eggs are shaped like the ones George Olsen found because they are laid in holes scooped out of the sand. There was another important fact. Only dinosaur bones were in this deposit. And anyway the Cretaceous birds, 70 million years ago, were much too small to have laid an eight-inch egg. Yes, it seemed quite certain these must be dinosaur eggs.

The three lying on the ground had broken out of a

shelf of sandstone. It was slowly crumbling through the action of weathering. We could see pieces of broken shell and the ends of several other eggs in the rock. Dr. Granger said it would be best to take up the whole block of sandstone just as it was. At the Museum the other eggs could be worked out carefully.

Then we had another surprise. As he started to brush away the loose sediment on top of the eggs, he exposed the skeleton of a small dinosaur! It was only two or three feet long and had no teeth. Later Professor Osborn found it to be a new kind of dinosaur. He named it Oviraptor (*O-vi-rap'-tor*) which means "the egg stealer." He believed it had lived by sucking the eggs of other dinosaurs. Probably it was in the act of digging up the eggs when a sudden windstorm buried it right on top of the nest it had meant to rob.

Months later I was in the Museum when the block of sandstone arrived. It was like opening a Christmas package. Bit by bit the rock was chipped away. In the center of the stone, lay thirteen beautiful eggs in a circle of two layers. Their ends pointed inward. We could see pieces of white bone through breaks in the shell of two eggs. When they were opened, the skeletons of unhatched baby dinosaurs were exposed. So there could no longer

Baby dinosaurs as they may have looked coming from eggs.

be any doubt about these being dinosaur eggs.

A few days after the first discovery, five eggs were found in a cluster. Also another group of nine. When we left the Flaming Cliffs, we had twenty-five eggs.

In the summer of 1925, the expedition again returned to the Flaming Cliffs. We had the feeling that more eggs and more skeletons might be discovered. I knew we had found all that were exposed in 1923. Our paleontologists had combed the ground foot by foot. Granger, Olsen and the others did not miss fossils. They were not that kind of men.

But two winters of wind and frost and icy gales had blasted the cliffs. One summer of fiercely hot days and cold nights had split the rocks. In some places a year or two makes little difference. In others it may produce great changes in the surface of the ground. We hoped that the Flaming Cliffs was such a place. It was.

There were more dinosaur eggs—eggs of different kinds from any we had found the first year. The weathering had worked a miracle in that soft red sandstone. It had swept the sand from the surface of hundreds of feet of rock and cliff. In some spots only half an inch of sand had been removed. Still that was enough to expose a tiny bit of shell or the tip of a white bone.

All About Dinosaurs

"Bigger and better eggs" was our slogan. Almost every man in camp hunted eggs from morning till night. I found several as did all the others. But George Olsen became the champion dinosaur egg hunter of the world. He had amazing success.

One day he saw a tiny piece of shell in the loose sand. A few yards away was another bit, then no more. Crawling on his hands and knees, he looked over every inch of ground. No sign of eggs. Impatiently, he struck his little pickax into a crack in the rock. As he pulled it out, he overturned a chunk weighing fifty pounds. On the underside were four dinosaur eggs, three of them unbroken. These are small and have smooth surfaces. They are now in the Chicago Museum of Natural History.

Olsen made another discovery of an even dozen eggs, larger and finer than any of the others. They had broken from a low shelf of rock and were lying buried in soft sand. All he had to do was to brush them out. These eggs are almost perfectly elliptical and about nine inches long. The shells are one-eighth of an inch thick and very solid.

But another group found by Dr. Loucks had shells of almost paper thinness. They are only four inches long and very slender with pointed ends. There is a smooth-shelled type a little larger. Also two still bigger varieties

One nest of dinosaur eggs was found on this cliff.

with pebbled shells. Without doubt these represent different kinds of dinosaurs. Probably the smaller ones were laid by the little flesh-eating dinosaurs whose bones we found. The larger eggs were certainly the product of Protoceratops andrewsi.

One nest was discovered by Norman Lovell in a most peculiar way. He saw an eagle's nest near the top of a cliff, two hundred feet above the basin floor. It might contain young birds, and he wanted them for pets. Crawling on his stomach along the very rim of the cliff, he scratched his hand on something sharp. It was the knife-like edge of a broken dinosaur egg shell! Fourteen eggs were partly exposed, lying in a circle. Again this was pure luck, for Lovell was only thinking of the eagle's nest. It was a very difficult and dangerous job to remove the dinosaur eggs. A high wind blew the whole time, and Walter Granger had to work while lying at full length. I was afraid he might fall over the edge of the cliff and be killed.

Many bits of eggshell were scattered over the ground in the basin. Dr. Chaney picked up 750 pieces in one afternoon. It was quite plain that dinosaurs had come here in great numbers to lay their eggs.

In this region our geologists found chunks of fossil

The skull of a dinosaur as it was found in sand and rock.

wood like those of a desert tree. They decided that 70 million years ago this valley was as dry as it is today. Probably the very fine loose sand was just right for hatching dinosaur eggs.

How were the eggs preserved? This is the way it must have been. The "hen" dinosaur scooped out a shallow hole and laid her eggs. Then she spread a thin covering of sand over them. This ended the job so far as she was concerned. She didn't sit on her eggs, like a chicken, to keep them warm. The sun did that. But, of course, the sand had to be loose and porous so air and heat could get to the eggs. The little dinosaurs must breathe through the air holes in the shell like a bird. Probably during a windstorm, many feet of sand were heaped over some of the nests. That cut off warmth and air. The eggs never hatched. As time went on, more and more sand piled up. Finally it became so heavy that the shells cracked, and the liquid contents ran out. At the same time, sand sifted into the shells and made a core. That kept the eggs in their original shape. After many thousands of years the sand over the eggs was pressed together into rock.

The Gobi Desert is the only place in the world where dinosaur eggs have been discovered. In Rognac, France, a small piece of shell may possibly be from a dinosaur egg, but it is only a fragment. Conditions had to be exactly right to preserve such delicate things as eggs. Undoubtedly other places had those conditions, but they have not been found so far.

The Gobi Desert eggs created a great deal of interest all over the world. Newspapers published thousands of words about them. But everybody was disappointed because they are so small. People usually think of dinosaurs only as the great Sauropods, like Brontosaurus. They do not understand that there were big dinosaurs and small ones, just as there are big reptiles and little ones today. Protoceratops was a small dinosaur only eight or nine feet long. Well, if an eight-foot dinosaur lays an eight-inch egg, that is not such a bad effort! An inch of egg to a foot of dinosaur! Some day an egg of Brontosaurus, or one of the great dinosaurs may be discovered. That would satisfy everybody, for it would probably be as large as a football.

The Flaming Cliffs proved to be the most important single fossil locality in the entire world. It gave us Proto-ceratops, the ancestor of the horned dinosaurs. It gave us the dinosaur eggs. It gave us the earliest known mammals.

FLYING DRAGONS
AND SEA SERPENTS

Although dinosaurs were lords of the land, flying reptiles ruled the air. Thousands upon thousands swarmed
through the sky in the Mesozoic period. They are called
pterodactyls (*ter-o-dack'-tils*) which means "wing finger." Some were very big, and some were hardly larger
than a sparrow. There were pterodactyls with long tails;
pterodactyls with short tails and pterodactyls with no
tails at all. Some flew by day; others flew at night. At
least we think they did, because of their owl-like eyes.

All About Dinosaurs

None of them had feathers. Instead, their skins were naked and quite smooth. The smaller ones probably lived on insects, catching them in the air like bats. The big ones of the Cretaceous period scooped up fish in their long beaks.

In all the pterodactyls, each wing was formed by a sheet of skin stretched on the long "little" finger back to the hind leg. That isn't a very good wing, for the reptile couldn't fly if the skin were torn. The bat's wing is supported by four fingers which spread the wing skin apart and strengthen it. In birds, of course, the finger bones are bound closely together to hold the feathers of the wing. The pterodactyls probably sailed and glided more than actually flapping their wings.

Pteranodon (*Ter-an'-o-don*) of the Cretaceous period was the biggest of all the flying reptiles. He was a fantastic, goblin-like creature. I always think of him as a witch on a broomstick that sailed through the sky. He had a long beak, with no teeth, and a great triangular cap or crest. It looked something like a fish's fin. Possibly it acted as a rudder to steer the reptile as it soared through the air.

Although the wings were more than 20 feet long, the body was very small. Probably Pteranodon did not weigh as much as a large turkey. The bones were hollow like those of a bird so they must have been light. Actually the bones were no thicker than a post card. Therefore, they were smashed flat in most fossil skeletons and are difficult to put together.

The remains of Pteranodon have been found mostly in the fine sediment of the chalk beds of western Kansas. These were formed far out in the great inland sea that then occupied the state of Kansas. The chalk beds are more than 100 miles from what was the nearest shore-line at that time. So Pteranodon must have gone out at least 100 miles over the water.

People who make airplanes have studied the way this great flying reptile was built. The mechanics of his wings are not good. Birds and bats have much better wings for true flight. Pteranodon couldn't do a "power dive" because the wings could not be folded backward. It would be impossible to change speed quickly.

But Pteranodon must have been a very fine glider. He could soar majestically through the sky, up and down, back and forth. All he had to do was to take advantage of the air currents rising from the warm tropical land or water below him. When feeding, he probably glided along just above the water, and darted his long bill into the waves to pick up a fish that was near the surface.

How remains of Pteranodon happen to be preserved is a real mystery. The body was so very light that it must have floated. After a while the bones must have fallen apart. But almost complete skeletons have been found. A fine one is in the American Museum of Natural History. Another in the Yale University Museum shows the imprint of the wing membrane. It seems possible that when a Pteranodon was gliding close to the surface, it might have been seized by a fish or a sea reptile. The hollow bones would be broken and filled with water. If the fish did not eat the Pteranodon at once, the remains would sink to the bottom. There it might be buried in the soft mud. That is about the only explanation that has been presented.

All the pterodactyls had large brains for reptiles. Their sight was very good and the sense of smell poor. This is like our present-day birds. The flying reptiles needed good eyes, and big ones, for they were high up in the air and had to chase their prey by sight.

How Pteranodon moved on land is not clear. He might rest upon the knuckle joints of the closed wings, but he couldn't walk on them. The wing joints were not able to move forward or back. If he stood on his hind

Protoceratops andrewsi was one of the ugliest of dinosaurs.

legs, the wings must have been held uplifted. Probably this big glider didn't walk at all. There were three hooked claws on the wing joints. They could be used to hold on to trees and rocks. He could land on a cliff or high rock and hang there to rest. When he wanted to fly again, he simply pushed himself off into the air. We have no information and not even good guesses about their nests or their young.

Sea Serpents

While pterodactyls swept along the surface of Mesozoic seas, marine reptiles that were not dinosaurs swarmed in the water below them. Of course, some of the dinosaurs did go into the water. As you know, the Thunder Lizard and its cousin Diplodocus spent much of their time splashing about in the mud and shallows of lakes and rivers. The Duckbill dinosaurs were good swimmers. But they were really land animals.

The reptiles I am writing about lived in the water all the time, and never came out on land. The best known is the great Plesiosaur (*Plees'-i-o-sawr*). He had a long snake-like neck, small head, jaws full of sharp teeth, a body like a turtle and a good sized tail. He fits perfectly the popular idea of a sea serpent.

All About Dinosaurs

When vacations start in the summer, many city people go to the shore. Then sea serpent stories are sure to be published in the newspapers. The sea is a mysterious place. People like to believe that strange, ancient creatures still exist in the unexplored ocean. Why can't it be true?

Well, nothing is impossible in nature. But the modern sea serpent idea is improbable. So many ships travel across every ocean that even the greatest depths have been explored. If big unknown creature like Plesiosaurs still lived, they would be seen by many people. Some would certainly die and their bodies would drift ashore.

Dead sea serpents are often reported. I have followed up some of these stories myself. Always they prove to be basking sharks, whales, sea lions or some other animal well known to scientists.

One widespread sea serpent story was about the "Loch Ness Monster" of Scotland. Many people saw what they thought was its long neck and part of its body above the surface of the water. Tracks of huge webbed feet were said to have been seen in the mud. A man actually photographed the monster. That did it. The picture was sent to The New York *Times*. They brought it to me at the American Museum of Natural History. The "neck" of the monster proved to be the high, slender back fin of a killer whale.

So it is with most of the sea-serpent stories. People see some strange creature. They have only a quick view of it and imagine the rest. At present there is no reason to believe that any of the great marine reptiles of the Age of Reptiles still exist. So far as we know, they died out with the dinosaurs millions of years ago.

There were many kinds of Plesiosaurs. The seas of the Jurassic and Cretaceous periods were full of them. Some were big and some were small, but none was fish-like in form or habits. They lived more like turtles but did not wear a shell. Probably the skin was smooth and

Giant turtles lived in the sea in the days of dinosaurs.

naked. Their broad, flat bodies had strong paddles on either side which were used like oars. The joints and muscle attachments show that they could row backward as well as forward. When such a creature met a fish, his slender neck could shoot out like a striking snake. Once the fish was in its mouth, the long sharp teeth held it like a trap.

Plesiosaurs lived entirely in the water. It is doubtful that they ever came out on land. Instead they paddled placidly along near shore. There they could see the gigantic Thunder Lizards wading in the shallows, stuffing trailing water plants into their mouths. They could see small running dinosaurs skipping over the rocks and witness furious battles between big flesh-eaters like Allosaurus. From the safety of the water they had a good view of dinosaur life. What a movie it would have made!

Terror in the Sea

The inland sea of Kansas was a sad place for the smaller creatures that lived in its waters. Gigantic reptiles, mosasaurs (*mo'-sa-sawrs'*), roamed the depths. In it swam the King of Turtles, Archelon (*Ark'-e-lon*). He was a dozen feet or more in length, with a head a full yard long. In the shallows prowled huge fish with massive jaws and teeth like spikes. Over the water, pterodactyls sailed majestically, ready to snap up surface-feeding creatures. Truly those were troublesome times for the small fry of the old Kansas sea!

Hundreds, or even thousands, of bones of mosasaurs have been taken from the chalk beds. The mosasaurs were really swimming lizards that grew to great size. Some were as long as 30 feet and distantly related to the living varanus lizards of Asia and Africa. The largest of the mosasaurs, Tylosaurus (*Tile'-o-sawr'-us*) was as big as a small whale. It probably weighed more than a Duckbill dinosaur. Tylosaurus was completely water-living and never came out on land. The long flexible body, powerful tail, and paddle-shaped feet could push it through the water at great speed. The mouth was filled with terrifying rows of sharp-pointed teeth for holding slippery fish. That Tylosaurus gulped his food is shown by the bones of the lower jaw. Each jaw is hinged in the middle and can be bowed outward. This gives the creature a much larger mouth.

Mosasaurs fit the idea of a sea serpent pretty well. Unfortunately, there is no reason to believe that they still exist. Their day was during the Cretaceous period, 70 million years ago.

All About Dinosaurs

The inland seas were shallow, and after a while the land began to lift up. The movement was very slow, perhaps only an inch or two in a century, but it continued to rise. Finally, hills and ridges in the sea bottom pushed up to the surface. They formed islands and sand bars. These kept getting bigger and cut the sea into lakes. After millions of years, these too disappeared. When they dried up, the reptiles caught in those inland seas died. But while they lived, they lived well.

Ichthyosaurs

These reptiles were completely fish-like in form. The modern shark, the modern porpoise, and the ancient ichthyosaur (*ik'-thee-o-sawr'*) all were shaped alike. That was because they lived the same kind of life in the water, and they had to adapt themselves to it. From the outside, you might think all of them were fish. But underneath the skin, the body structure tells the story. The shark is shown to be a fish; the porpoise is a mammal and the ichthyosaur is unmistakably a reptile. It had the reptile's muscles and bone and brain, and the reptile's heart and lungs.

None of the ichthyosaurs got to be nearly as large as the mosasaur, Tylosaurus. Most of them were only 10

Ichthyosaurus was 10 to 15 feet long.

or 15 feet long. The body was streamlined for fast movement in the water. The head was sharp pointed, the tail two-lobed, and the four legs were like fins. It also had a high back fin. This kept the animal from rolling from side to side as it swam. Sharp teeth for holding fish filled the mouth. The eyes were very large.

Reptiles are egg-laying animals. Since the ichthyosaurs were reptiles, but never came out on land, how were the young born? Nature seems to have taken care of that. Instead of laying eggs in a nest as dinosaurs did, they kept them within their bodies. When the eggs hatched, the young appeared alive. In scientific language, they were ovoviviparous (*o-vo-vi-vip'-ar-ous*).

We are pretty sure this is true, because of an ichthyosaurus skeleton in the American Museum of Natural History. This came from Holzmaden, Germany, a little town near Stuttgart. The reptile lies in a slab of slate, 9 feet long and 2½ feet wide. It is perfectly preserved, and in the body cavity are the skeletons of several young animals. The baby ichthyosaurs are surprisingly large. The head of one is 9½ inches long. That is half as large as the mother's head. The backbone and paddles of the babies are well developed and show that they could swim as soon as born.

All About Dinosaurs

So here is a wonderful adaptation for life in the water. It is evident that ichthyosaurs were once land-living reptiles and laid their eggs in the sand as others do. At that time, they did not have bodies shaped like a fish. But for some unknown reason, they began to spend more and more time in the water. So they became fish-like in shape and had to change their way of having babies, too, since they could not go out on land.

Not only do we know how ichthyosaurs gave birth to their young but also how they looked in life. This is because another remarkable specimen was discovered in the slate quarries at Holzmaden, Germany. It shows the outline of the body, fins, paddles and tail, as a black film in slate. This is one of the most remarkable fossils ever found.

In this chapter I have written about only a few of the reptiles that lived in the air and in the sea when dinosaurs ruled the land. There were others, but they were smaller and not so spectacular. Giant sharks and turtles and crocodiles were there, too, but this book is only about the reptiles of the Mesozoic Era.

DEATH OF THE DINOSAURS

Why did dinosaurs become extinct? We don't know. We are only sure that they did. It may have been caused by a combination of circumstances. No one of them alone would have been enough to kill off all the dinosaurs, but taken together they did the job. It happened at the end of the Cretaceous period, with dramatic suddenness, geologically speaking. Probably the most important factor was a change in physical conditions. Our modern mountain systems were not born at that time.

All About Dinosaurs

The world-wide tropical climate of Mesozoic days was being replaced by temperate and cold areas. The hot humid lowlands gave way to rolling uplands. Hardwood forests grew where palm and fig trees had flourished in the jungle.

Of course these changes did not take place quickly as we conceive it. It was thousands upon thousands of years before they could be really noticed. But they continued just a little year by year. After a while the dinosaurs began to feel it. Lakes, rivers, and marshes, where the big vegetable feeders splashed about, became smaller and smaller. It was difficult to get food enough to fill their stomachs. Their huge bodies were too big to move far. Since they couldn't change their eating habits, they died.

That was fatal for the flesh-eating dinosaurs which lived upon the vegetable feeders. They lost their food supply. Big fellows like the King of Tyrants needed tons of meat to keep them alive. Even a fat Duckbill would last only a meal or two. These dinosaurs were what is called too highly "specialized." Their bodies had become adapted to a special kind of life and climate and food, and they couldn't live any other way. They were unable to meet the new conditions.

Other reasons, too, may have helped the dinosaurs to

become extinct. There is what is called "racial senescence" which means "old age of the race." The dinosaurs may have died because they were old and had reached the end of their rope.

This kind of old age is sometimes shown by the production of strange forms. Such, for instance, as some of the armored dinosaurs, with spines and projections and bumps and warts all over their bodies. Racial old age

The giant Stegosaurus had a brain the size of a kitten's.

might have been responsible for the death of a few kinds of dinosaurs, but not of the whole group.

Possibly an important reason was the very small and poor brain of these great reptiles. In Stegosaurus, which must have weighed four or five tons, the brain was no larger than that of a small kitten. With such a brain, the animal could barely eat and sleep and muddle through life. The Thunder Lizard and the other great Sauropods were not much better off in brain capacity.

Near the end of the Age of Reptiles, the warm-blooded mammals began to appear. These were tiny little furry fellows, no larger than a rat. At the Flaming Cliffs we found skulls and skeletons of eight of these little mammals. It is quite possible that they ate the dinosaur eggs. Thus, many dinosaurs were never born. This must have happened in many parts of the world. It could be one of the causes, but only one, of why dinosaurs became extinct.

Perhaps competition with the active, large-brained mammals became too great. The cold-blooded dinosaurs were too sluggish and too stupid to hold their place in nature.

Still one would think that some dinosaurs might have survived, that the smaller forms could have adapted themselves to changing conditions. But they did not.

Another question. Why did the great marine reptiles like the mosasaurs, plesiosaurs, and ichthyosaurs die with the dinosaurs? They had existed in many seas that did not dry up. Why could they not continue to live in the water as well as our present-day whales? But they all disappeared at the end of the Age of Reptiles. So did the pterodactyls, the "flying dragons."

We can only guess why this happened. The life cycle of all animals seems to be determined by nature. When they have lived their allotted span, they die. Dinosaurs were the biggest, the most fantastic and the most terrible creatures that ever walked the earth. They reached majestic heights, but the only record that they ever lived at all is in their bones enclosed in the enduring rock.

INDEX

Index

Index

Allabout Books

T.W. VOTER

This title was originally catalogued by the Library of Congress as follows:

Andrews, Roy Chapman, 1884–
    All about dinosaurs; illustrated by Thomas W. Voter.
New York, Random House ₁1953₎
    146 p. illus. 24 cm. (Allabout books)

    1. Dinosauria. 2. Paleontology—Juvenile literature.   ɪ. Title.

QE862.D5A5   568.19   53—6278 ‡

    Library of Congress   ₁67w³⁴₁₎

Trade Ed.: ISBN: 0-394-80201-2   Lib. Ed.: ISBN: 0-394-90201-7